SO-EIH-863

PUBLISHED BY SUSAN M. ORSEN
PRINTS PUBLISHING
BOX 387
VICTORIA, MINNESOTA 55386-0387
(612) 443-2010

PRINTS OF A PRIEST by Father Elstan Coghill, O.F.M.
©1996. 209 pages. Color photos. $16.95.
Says the author: "There's this book (note spelling, P-R-I-N-T-S)
written by a priest who is not equipped to compete
with St. Augustine, Thomas Aquinas, Socrates, Plato, or
Aristotle -- so he just put down on paper
a number of his experiences, events, acquaintances, and a few
other items that don't fall under any of these categories, in the hope
people will enjoy them. The only way you will ever know
is by buying the book and reading it."

THE VICTORIA GAZETTE.
Since 1979. Annual subscription, $10.
This monthly newspaper is read from "cover to cover"
by people from across the nation, many of whom don't know
a living or dead soul in Victoria, Minnesota. But thousands
seem to fall in love with the place -- and the people -- when they
read the Gazette. In any case, it's recyclable.

VOICES ARE CALLING by Jesse Coghill.
©1997. 113 pages. Black/White photography. $15.
Written for "the common man," the poetry in VOICES was
conceived in the golden years of a country fellow. The book
might have been brought to you sooner, but the author had to,
first, work to make a living and,
second, find a publisher who cared more about him and his poetry
than making a living.

PACKAGING AND POSTAGE ($3) AND SALES TAX (6½%)
MUST ALWAYS BE INCLUDED WHEN ORDERING THE BOOKS.
OR ASK FOR THEM AT YOUR FAVORITE BOOKSTORE.

VOICES
ARE CALLING

VOICES ARE CALLING

Poetry For The Common Man

By Jesse Coghill

VOICES ARE CALLING
Poetry For The Common Man

©1997 Jesse Coghill.
All rights reserved. No part of this book may be reproduced
in any form without permission from the publisher.

Published in the United States of America by
Susan M. Orsen
PRINTS PUBLISHING
Post Office Box 387
Victoria, MN 55386-0387

Susan M. Orsen, Editor, Photographer, Cover Design.

Library of Congress Catalog Card Number: 97-69815
ISBN 0-9652263-1-X

Dedication

I can't dedicate this book of poetry to my dad because he died before imparting much knowledge to me.

I can't dedicate it to my brother because he left home while I was very young and we didn't completely bond.

So I'll have to dedicate it to the women in my life --
- to the teachers and nuns who showered me with verbal abuse on a daily basis.
- to a mother who was wrapped up with her own problems and grief after Dad died.
- to an older sister who was too bossy for her own good.
- to a wife who is seldom completely happy or totally satisfied with anything.

At the same time, however, I admit that all of the above are or were an important part of my life, for they provided the ingredients that made me what I am today -- a poet, a dreamer, and a rebel.

Might I also acknowledge the Almighty? He blessed me with good health, a fertile mind, some imagination, and a heck of a lot of fun doing the rhyming thing.

-- *Jesse Coghill*

The wanderlust is a sacred trust;
It can maim you and it can kill.
But the voices keep calling, calling to me,
Those voices that won't be still.

Foreword

When the lawn is cut, the vegetable garden weeded, and the wife tenderly tended, what's an old man to do? Jesse Coghill listens to voices and writes poetry.

Born and raised -- and still living and breathing -- on a farm near Jordan, Minnesota, Jesse Coghill writes poetry for the common man. Jesse will tell you his poetry is for the common man because he himself is a common man. I tell you, however, that Jesse is uncommonly common. How many old men do you know who write stories in rhyme? Who put words of the heart and soul on paper? Who surrender thoughts of today, yesterday, and tomorrow to others? Jesse Coghill does.

His poetry does speak to us, the common man. Within it we find life as it could be, as it would be, as it sometimes is. Because his poetry is from the heart, it touches us. In some of it we see ourselves. In some of it we see others. In all of it we see Jesse Coghill, a man who has experienced good times and bad, who looks outside himself as well as inside, who ponders the world as he has seen it, imagined it, and lived it.

In VOICES ARE CALLING, Jesse Coghill writes of Friends and Foreigners, Nature and Beast, Battles and Blessings, Pen and Poetry, Youth and Old Age. His poetry is uncommonly good.

-- Sue Orsen, Publisher

P.S. Photographs were taken at the Coghill farm and at Jordan.

TABLE OF CONTENTS

POETRY
FOR THE
COMMON MAN

Friends and Foreigners

Now I won't judge my fellow man;
That certainly wouldn't be fair.
Just let the pearly gates swing wide
When I climb that golden stair.

The Northern Man

The trapper mushed through arctic night.
The moon cast down its cold pale light.
Stars were dancing heel and toe,
Creating diamonds on the snow.

Cold cut through his coat like a surgeon's knife;
He thought of warm cabins and also his wife.
His thoughts rambled on, as he made his round,
About lack of game and prices way down.

It grabbed his foot; he heard a snap.
He was caught in the jaws of a grizzly trap
Placed there last fall by Mountie Morse
To snare the rogue bear that killed his horse.

The trap wouldn't open -- the spring was too strong;
In this forty below weather he wouldn't last long.
He freed the chain from the anchor stake
And dragged himself 'cross the frozen lake.

The wolf pack sensed the wounded prey;
Cursing and shouting kept them at bay.
The going got harder with every breath,
But he knew if he stopped he'd freeze to death.

On he went through the bitter night,
With finally the light of his cabin in sight.
In ultimate effort he crawled through the door,
And collapsed in a faint on the hardwood floor.

He awoke in a hospital far away,
Having been unconscious a night and a day.
He knew right away that something was wrong,
Then looked down and saw that his foot was gone.

Now a one-footed man can't work his line,
But he never was one to bitch and whine.
So he sold his traps and he sold his hides,
And moved to town as an armchair guide.

He talked of the land of the midnight sun
Where the musk ox roam and the wolf packs run,
Where the beavers work and the otters play --
Six months of night, six months of day.

He told tales of valleys, silent and deep,
Of the caribou herds and mountain sheep,
The streams full of fish -- you take them from shore --
Majestic mountains where the eagles soar.

Tourists came to listen and have a look;
His wife took notes and then wrote a book
Which sold quite well and was on TV,
Making money they thought they'd never see.

Now he lives out his days without care or need,
This old man of the north, the last of his breed.

The King of Hell

The royal pair toured the stinking slum,
Home to the poor and stench of scum.
No hope for the future, no hope of gain,
The king said, oh, how he felt their pain.

He assured them he would tell his staff
To raise some funds in their behalf.
Then with his jeweled and perfumed queen,
He sped off in his limousine.

At his palace home beyond the moor
He soon forgot about the poor.
In keeping with his princely state,
He sang and danced and drank and ate
And justified this raucous night,
"I am the king! This is my right!"

The rage of the poor would not abate --
They marched up to the castle gate.
They pushed aside the cowering guard
And poured en masse into the yard,
Raiding larders of bread and meat,
"Our children starve! They have to eat!"

Two of the poor then stealthily crept
Where the king in drunken stupor slept.
With daggers tightly in their hands
They sent him to the promised land.

St. Peter said, "Who's coming through?
There's no room here for men like you.
A hole in hell is where you'll be
To burn for all eternity."

The Immigrants

From the mountains they came,
From the farms and the towns,
To escape the oppression
Imposed by the crown.

To obtain precious freedom,
To worship as they please,
They paid for transportation
At a port of embarkation
And left on their long jouney
'Cross the vast and open sea.

They endured many trials
On that filth-ridden ship,
But they never lost hope
Throughout the whole trip.

They spied Miss Liberty
With torch in her hand
And all started smilin'
Upon Ellis Island
For at last they had reached
The great promised land.

They reveled in stories
That were told and retold
About milk and honey
And streets paved with gold.

Settled in neighborhoods
With men of their kind,
They continued the customs
That they'd left behind.

They worked in the factories,
They worked in the mines,
They worked in the mills
And on railroad lines.

Yes, they toiled and slaved
And down through the years
They built a great nation
With blood, sweat, and tears.

The Golden Goose

Mother, father, son, and daughter
Live by shining big sea water
In a house so big and roomy
On the shores of Gitchegoome.

When we make peace and sign the treaty,
Great White Father shook our hand
Then turned around and took our land,
Gather people from all nations,
Herd us onto reservations.

Many sick and many died;
White man's word is "genocide."
But legends tell from days of old,
One day we get the white man's gold.

Jackpot Junction, Mystic Lake,
Long Knife's money Indian take.
Plenty wampum all we need,
Credit to the white man's greed.

Now we have the golden goose,
Build fine schools for our papoose,
Drive nice cars, eat good food,
Indian never had so good.

As we reach our final goal,
Gain back all the white man stole.
He cut our trees and killed our bison,
But red man see a new horizon --
Soon own all of Minnesota,
Iowa, and both Dakotas.

We have great weapons, mighty tool;
Slot machine make wise man fool.
Only one thing more to say:
Do Indians really talk this way?

The Music Man

Playing great concert halls of the land,
He sold out crowds on one night stands.
Roaring ovations and press adulation
Called for encores time and again --
They loved music he made with his violin.

He played for royals on a European tour,
Notes floating out so mellow and pure;
Music of the Master flowed from his hands --
Beethoven, Strauss, Chopin and Brahms.

Sad to say he was cursed with terrible thirst;
Deep he fell into debauchery and sin.
People were saying, "It's affecting his playing.
Too many fast women and too much slow gin!"

Caught with a duke's wife at Chateau la France,
He barely escaped by the seat of his pants.
He ran to the airport for all he was worth,
And headed straight back to the land of his birth.

Reputation preceding, not hired to play,
Even old friends turned him away.
So he played for drinks in the honky tonk bar
And for coins that people tossed into his jar.

He sank lower and lower, till one day he died;
None came to his wake and nobody cried.
In an unmarked grave, with no next of kin,
He had the clothes on his back and his old violin.

People talked of his talent and the terrible waste,
And they too easily judged this poor man in haste.
What wonderful things might have happened to him
If not for fast women and too much slow gin.

The Irish Wedding

Roving 'round the Ring of Kerry
In the spring of eighty-three,
At a pub for some refreshments,
A fellow says to me:

"Me daughter's gettin' married
And I'd like you for my guest.
The service starts at ten o'clock,
So wear your Sunday best."

The church was filled to overflow;
They'd come from miles around,
All the way from Galway Bay
And even Dublin Towne.

The bride all sweet and dewy-eyed,
As pretty as a queen,
The groom so stiff and nervous
Gazing at his fair Colleen.

After Mass they stood embraced,
He even kissed her twice.
Outside they went to shaking hands
And throwing of the rice.

Congratulations over,
We retired to the hall
To eat our fill and have a drink
And start the wedding ball.

The food was so delicious;
The cooks had done it proud.
The Kerry dancers pranced around
To entertain the crowd.

Oh, the whiskey flowed like buttermilk
And Guiness from the kegs,
The way that we were drinking it
Filled all our hollow legs.

The fiddles started scrapin'
With the whistle of the flute,
On the floor the dainty slippers
Dancing next to ploughman's boot.

Through the singing and the laughin'
McCarthy played his fife;
Everything was going great
'Til Casey winked at Ryan's wife.

Outside they went to duke it out
And scuffle in the dirt;
It's fortunate for both of them
That neither one was hurt.

That's the way the party went
'Til far into the night,
And only started breakin' up
At dawning's early light.

So home we reeled o'er hill and field
To try to get some sleep;
Some would go to milk their cows
And some to tend their sheep.

For weeks it's all we talked about;
It was a grand affair.
And looking back upon it now
I'm glad that I was there.

The Brave Knight

Brave knight mounted on noble steed
Gallops away at breakneck speed.
His lady is captive in the enemy tower;
To her rescue -- and his finest hour!

Scale the wall in a leap and a bound,
She in his arms, he'll carry her down.
Off they will flee like the very wind;
This story will come to a happy end.

She screams, "I can't go in this terrible dress.
My lipstick's smeared, and my hair is a mess!
You have always been a thoughtless twit.
Why didn't you bring my make-up kit?"

"Come," he says, "we must make haste.
The guard's on my heels and my blood he tastes."
"Give me a break," she says, "Get wise!
I don't mind a little time here with these guys.

"At least now I'm getting all three squares
And a nice apartment at the top of the stairs.
So what if I warm that old man's bed?
A girl has to do things, Mom always said.

"Just look at your suit of rusty mail,
Chasing in search of the Holy Grail,
Spending your days on that smelly horse,
Paying alimony from your last divorce.

"Your ex is hauling your ass to court.
You're six months behind in child support.
And you want me to be your next wife?
I've news for you buster: Get a life!"

Back she ran across the bridge,
Up to her room and opened the fridge,
Cracked a beer and filled her glass --
Ah, life was good for the winsome lass.

His heart was so heavy, it split a seam
As he walked out into the rushing stream.
He was found on a sandbar, stiff and cold;
Life could be grim in the days of old.

A moral you ask? It must be this:
Never be fooled by a maiden's kiss.
The heroine's morals were rather loose,
And yet she found the golden goose.

Our knight, the poor fool, now stands at hell's gate,
Fornicated by the fickle finger of fate.

Oh, he was quite the little man,
With vest of green and shoes of tan,
Those twinkling eyes so full of guile,
The wrinkled brow and crooked smile.

The Leprechaun

While dreaming one morn just before dawn,
I met my old friend, the leprechaun.
"How are you, you little elf?"
"I'm just fine, sir, and how's yourself?"
He danced a jig around a thistle
While playing a tune on his penny whistle.
He bowed at waist and tipped his bonnet
And flashed a grin with mischief on it.
Oh, he was quite the little man,
With vest of green and shoes of tan,
Those twinkling eyes so full of guile,
The wrinkled brow and crooked smile.
He stole my milk and raided my garden,
Guess I will have to grant him pardon
For very much like the will-o-the-wisp,
He disappeared and drifted away
And I awakened on another day.

The Priest

He left for a life in the clergy,
Right out of parochial school.
He learned the priestly teachings,
He followed the priestly rule.

His day of ordination,
It seems so long ago.
He listened to his superiors,
Going where they told him to go.

Now in his golden years,
He no longer has to roam
For my brother's at St. Victoria,
Close to his boyhood home.

The Towheaded Kid

"Whatever happened to that towheaded kid?
He was Donald's oldest son."
"Haven't you heard? He's off in the seminary.
My wife was talking to his mum."
"What made him do a fool thing like that?
It takes so darn much study!"
"He'll be back in a couple of weeks.
Just mark my word, old buddy!"
"I didn't know he was a studious one,
reading books and such."
"Never seemed to like horses and farming,
at least not very much."

That was the talk sixty years ago,
and it hasn't changed to this day.
People who don't know what they're talking about
often have most to say.
We all have seen him stick it out,
that towheaded boy named Jim.
And you probably know who I'm talking about --
Father Elstan, O.F.M.

Whenever I can, I visit his grave,
So many memories I want to save --
His old straw hat, his sunburned brow,
Those big gnarled hands that guided the plow.

The Farmer

He hung up his pitchfork and moved into town,
But somehow he just could not settle down.
Out of bed with the sun, he surveyed his yard;
Nothing grows on cement -- it's just too damn hard.

Neighbors complained about the two goats
That he kept tied up on the lawn --
And also the old, cocky, red rooster
Who crowed at the cracking of dawn.

Threatened with arrest
By the law's long arm,
He packed it all up
And moved back to the farm.

He was too old and frail to be out there alone,
So his relatives had him put into a home.
Confined to four walls in a dimly lit room,
He died before light of the next full moon.

Whenever I can, I visit his grave,
So many memories I want to save --
His old straw hat, his sunburned brow,
Those big gnarled hands that guided the plow.

During the war those hands held a gun,
Then the softness of a newborn son.
His way of life gone, it just couldn't last --
Gone, too, is the link with our pioneer past.

The Missus

This is an ode to my wife LaVerne

Who's one hundred percent Bohemian sperm.

Five foot two and kind of sassy,

When all dressed up she's pretty classy.

She likes nice things that are expensive;

Her shopping sprees are darned extensive.

At cooking she is quite astute;

She also paints and plays the flute.

After all these years I've learned

I'm going to keep my wife LaVerne.

The Fools

There they stand in fond embrace,

Smooching, making kissy face.

I thought of him as my good friend;

And her, I'll never trust again.

My feelings hurt, they'll never mend,

And then after a little while

I realize they're both senile.

Forget the vows, break all the rules?

Those two old kissing senile fools!

The Unemployed

He had a job and life was good;
Things were going as they should.
Yes, life was made to be enjoyed,
But things change fast; he's unemployed.

They handed him his severance pay,
With all his bills it slipped away.
On unemployment compensation,
He's like others across the nation.

He passed out countless resumes,
Only to be turned away.
As he walked that lonely street,
He felt his skills were obsolete.

He lost his car; he lost his home
To the bank that held his hefty loan.
He couldn't afford to pay for classes;
At last he joined the homeless masses.

He lived from grub in garbage cans
And begged with trembling, outstretched hands.
He turned to drink, he turned to dope.
His pride was gone, he lost all hope.

One bitter night there on the street,
He froze his hands, he froze his feet,
Then slipped into his final sleep
And lay there in a lifeless heap.

They found him resting in that place,
A peaceful smile upon his face.
I hope that God will grant him grace
And take him to a better place.

VOICES ARE CALLING

Whenever life plays dirty tricks,
Some blame it all on politics.
The government that makes the rules
Is filled with crooks and run by fools.

Will it ever change? I cannot say.
It seems it's always been that way.
All we can do is hope and pray
That soon we'll see a better day.

The Sweepstakes Man

Super Bowl Sunday is here at last;
Excitement grips the land.
But you won't catch me watching TV;
I'm waiting for Ed McMahon.

What's that coming up the road?
It looks like a mini-van.
Sakes alive, it turned in the drive.
Could it be Ed McMahon?

I heard a knock and went to the door --
I didn't walk, I ran.
It was only a guy selling pots and pans.
It wasn't Ed McMahon.

I told him where he could put his wares,
And closed the door with a bang.
Then back to the couch to sit in a slouch,
Still waiting for Ed McMahon.

They had written to say I was close to winning;
I thought it was in the can.
I even bought some magazines.
You owe me, Ed McMahon!

A day wears on, my hopes are gone,
So is my grandiose plan.
But you know next year I'll be right here,
Waiting for Ed McMahon.

The Author Unknown

Here is a person fully grown,
Works at a job, never alone.
How can you say
Author Unknown?

Is he a handsome young fellow
Or a crippled old crone,
This person you call
Author Unknown?

He has a wife and some children
Who are out on their own
This guy you call
Author Unknown.

He pays most of his bills
Plus interest on a loan,
And yet you insist he's
Author Unknown.

Off to work every morning,
At night he comes home,
One of the faceless masses,
Our Author Unknown.

He catches colds and the flu
And gets aches in his bones.
He's really kind of human,
This Author Unknown.

Hey, I know who he is,
It's so plain to see.
Our Author Unknown --
He's you and he's me.

The Booze Brain

He spent his nights in topless bars
And talked of sports and sex and cars.
With friends he guzzled ale and stout
And stayed until the lights went out.

With head so light and feet so heavy,
He crawled into his ancient Chevy,
Groped around to find a bottle,
Turned the key and hit the throttle.

Looking neither left nor right,
He roared into the stormy night.
The guardian angel at his side
Stayed with him on the risky ride.

When he rolled into his yard,
The angel said, "Boy, that was hard!
Guarding this guy is no fun.
Now I hope my job is done!"

Wife awaits with little children,
Temper boiling like a cauldron.
As he staggers up the path,
She unloads her pent-up wrath.

"Another night of drunken frolic,
You hopeless, useless alcoholic!
If you don't quit, then I'll be leaving
And you'll be all alone and grieving.

"No one to clean your pissed up bed,
No one to see you're proper fed.
No one to hear your drunken snore
Or wipe your vomit off the floor."

While her anger she's unloading,
His booze brain is fair exploding.
He stands there in a shameful crouch,
Then stumbles over to the couch.

His wife says, "Lord, on high above,
Are you the man I used to love?
I won't take this another day!
Tomorrow you must join A.A.!"

He wakes next day in terrible pain --
Ultimatum burns his brain --
Calls and gets a cheerful greeting,
That night goes to his first meeting.

Now when they walk past the bars,
She recalls the aching scars,
But winks at him with twinkling eye,
And arm in arm they stroll right by.

The Grace of God

The town drunk weaved and staggered by
As gossips cast a jaundiced eye
And stared at him so horrified.
There but for the grace of God go I.

On crutches shuffling down the street,
With shriveled legs and lifeless feet,
While stepping off the curb he fell --
To suffer this must be pure hell.
Give him credit, folks, he tried.
There but for the grace of God go I.

All she owns fills two shopping bags,
Her hair unkempt, her clothes are rags.
What caused this soul to sink so low?
None of us may ever know.
On lonely bench she heaves a sigh.
There but for the grace of God go I.

Let's have compassion, my good friends;
We don't know what the future sends.
Life's but a twinkling of the eye.
There but for the grace of God go I.

The Divorced

Just look at that wino
In a drunken trance,
Those yellow stains
Where he wet his pants,
His bloodshot eyes,
That purple nose,
Unwashed hair,
And greasy clothes.

He marched with Patton
During the war,
Wounded and decorated
In forty-four.
Did real well
When he got discharged;
Bought a big house
And a brand new car.

Then his wife divorced him.

She took it all,
Including the kids,
And after that
He hit the skids.
Now there he sits
All pale and thin;
God only knows
What might have been.

The Grouse

'Twas the night before Christmas and old Mister Grouse
Went out in the dark to his little outhouse.

He grunted and groaned as he worked at his chore;
Then suddenly came a loud knock at the door.

He spied through the half-moon a plump little chap
And yelled, "Go away! I'm taking a crap!"

The elf said, "Believe me, I'd sure like to go
But I'm up to my ass in three feet of snow.

"Half my reindeer are sick -- there's a bunch of no-shows.
Even Rudolph at home has a red runny nose."

Mister Grouse hollered, "Please! Quit gadding about!
I'll go find a shovel and help dig you out."

They shoveled and shoveled to no avail;
The sleigh remained stuck like a train off its rail.

Grouse said, "Put those beasts in the barn with some hay.
We'll finish this job by the light of the day."

So they went to the house to get out of the snow
And warmed their old bones by the fire's soft glow.

And then out of nowhere, there did appear
A feast fit for a king and kegs of cold beer.

They ate and they drank as the time just flew by.
Nick finished his route on the Fourth of July.

VOICES ARE CALLING

The Grim Reaper

The Grim Reaper gets us all;
Not one escapes his wrath.
But God will tell if it's heaven or hell
When we come to the end of our path.

"You, sir, you robbed and killed.
You cheated on your wife.
I guess you know you're going below
For you lived an immoral life.

"And there stands an evil monarch
Who caused many thousands of deaths.
I'm sending him down to that fiery town
To burn with all of the rest.

"But over here stand some common folks,
Hard working women and men,
Who've had their share of hell on earth --
To them I say, 'Come on in.'"

Now I won't judge my fellow man;
That certainly wouldn't be fair.
Just let the pearly gates swing wide
When I climb that golden stair.

Nature and Beast

Storm clouds billow in the western sky,
Looking down on the earth with an evil eye.
Lightning bolts, like a fiery rod,
Unleashing the wrath of an angry god.

Of Royal Stock

It stands upon a gentle rise,
Branches stretching toward the skies,
Solid as Gibraltar's Rock,
Its seed was born of royal stock.

Cyclone winds or winter snow,
None of these could lay it low;
Raging flood, searing drought --
These could never take it out.

What stories you would tell, old tree,
If only you could talk to me.
You'd tell me tales 'bout days of old,
How you watched events unfold.

You'd talk of wartime's terrible cost,
Of victories won and battles lost.
Beneath your boughs we found romance --
Did you smile a bit perchance?

Pioneers rested in your shade,
And cleared the land with ax and spade.
You heralded reapers that cut the grain,
The motor car and the aeroplane.

And yet you stand there tall and strong,
Listening to my poet heart's song.
You'll still be there, you sly old knave,
When I lie dead in my cold, cold grave.

Mister Tree

Joyce Kilmer wrote that only
God can make a tree --
I wholeheartedly agree.

Leaves with various
Hues of green,
Like crown jewels
Of a stately queen.

Birds and bees
Make homes in branches;
Ants use trunks
For little ant ranches.

When fall brings
The killing frost,
The green of leaves
Is quickly lost,

Replaced by oranges,
Reds, and gold --
Mister Tree, you're
A sight to behold!

Soon bitter north winds
Will strip your limbs bare.
You stand unconcerned,
You don't seem to care.

You won't feel soft raindrops,
Nor hear the birds sing,
So sleep the long sleep now,
Awaken in spring.

Morning Storm

Storm clouds billow in the western sky,
Looking down on the earth with an evil eye.
Lightning bolts, like a fiery rod,
Unleashing the wrath of an angry god.
It skips and dances across the land
And runs with the devil, hand in hand.
Out in the woods in one awesome stroke
It snuffs out the life of a mighty oak.
Thunder rolls like a celestial drummer
Marching ahead of the storms of summer.
Trees bend over in gales of wind,
Straighten up tall and bend again.
Then comes the dreaded pounding hail,
Beating out tunes on an old tin pail.
The winds subside, the clouds move on;
As fast as it came, the storm is gone.
The whole thing's over, and it's barely noon.
Ah, what is so rare as a day in June!

Mega Storm of '91

This year winter
Came to stay
On Halloween
And All Saints Day.
We stayed inside
Our cozy house
And watched the blizzard
Roar and grouse
And huff and puff
And rage and blow
The whirling, swirling
Driven snow.
Like animals
Who with their mates
Go to their dens
To hibernate,
We sit with cat
And woolen socks
To await the Vernal
Equinox.

Flood of '93

The Mississippi burst its seams,
Fed by rivers, lakes, and streams
That no longer could contain
Relentless and incessant rain
Spreading out on good rich soil,
Wiping out the farmers' toil.
Main Street businesses closed down,
Homes were flooded, people drowned.
When Mother Nature shows she's boss,
Then human nature takes the loss.
Let's hope that we never see
Another flood like '93.

Summer Night Sounds

Sometimes as I go to bed,
Putting down a book I read,
I listen to the sounds of night,
After turning out the light.

Semis jump and jam their gears,
I hear them on the highway.
Jumbo jets roar overhead
On mapped and spacious flyway.

Rustles of the soft warm breeze
Whisper to the slumbering trees.
A raccoon rummages, sly and intense;
A tomcat sings off key on the fence.

In the distance a dog is barking;
Is it due to illegal parking?
The guy up the road pulls into his drive
As his wife steps out and gives him some gibe.

"I suppose you've been hanging around with that bimbo
At the No-Tell Motel," she yells from the window.
"I worked overtime and didn't stop at that dive!"
"Then how come you reek of Chanel Number Five?"

It soon settles down until all that I hear
Are dozens of tiny tree frogs croaking near
And also the crickets -- "Cheep, cheep, cheep" --
As I'm drifting off into deep peaceful sleep.

VOICES ARE CALLING

Minnesota Nice

Eighteen hundred fifty-eight,
That's when we became a state,
Famous Minnesota nice,
Crappies, carp, and wild rice.

Proud of our ten thousand lakes,
Swamps and frogs and garter snakes,
State bird loons with calls that beckon,
Mosquitoes running a close second.

Fertile ground for corn and beans,
Pollution in our lakes and streams,
Taxes keep the whole thing going,
Metro area won't quit growing.

No one leaves for North Dakota;
Three rousing cheers for Minnesota!

Widow Kelley's Cat

The widow Kelley had a cat --
I'd like to say a bit on that.
The cat was black and plump and shaggy;
Mrs. Kelley called her Maggie.

All day she lounged around the house,
At night outside to catch a mouse
Or scare the birds or chase the squirrels --
The best of both the feline worlds.

They were to each other dear.
Weeks and months slipped into years
'Til one day Mrs. Kelley died,
The faithful Maggie by her side.

Friends and kin did what it takes
To have a proper Irish wake.
But as the coffin rolled out the door
What did they spy upon the floor?

All stretched out in sweet repose,
One tiny paw across its nose,
In final slumber on its favorite mat,
'Twas the corpse of Mrs. Kelley's cat!

Miss Kitty Wins Again

Miss Kitty ran to her warm soft nest
To slumber as cats know how to best.

A comely canine, rolly polly pup,
Yipped and whined and woke Miss Kitty up.
She stared and hissed, "No! I don't want to play.
I need my beauty rest. Please go away!"

He wouldn't give up, so she finally gave in
And crawled from her bed to call forth a game:
"You go now and hide in the laundry room
But don't come out till I call your name."

So all afternoon he stayed in the dark
And chewed on a pair of scruffy old shoes.
Kitty went back to her bed in a box,
Continuing on in slumbering snooze.

Late in the day the mistress came home;
She picked up the cat and gave her a pat
And mused from the chair in which she sat,
"I wonder where that puppy is at."

Miss Kitty purred as she groomed her fur
And gazed at the laundry room door.
The mistress yelled as she opened it,
"You naughty dog! You messed on the floor!"

Puppy was punished, his supper withheld --
He didn't receive a single crumb --
While Kitty was fed and went back to bed.
Does anyone think that cats are dumb?

Old Winter Thing

The furnace is humming,
The warm air is coming
Up through the vents in the wall.
Outside the wind is picking up,
And light snow is starting to fall.

Once more we enter
The season called winter
When everything slows down in pace.
And when taking a walk
It's quite hard to talk
With a scarf wrapped all 'round your face.

Last night in the moonlight
Some deer found our lawn --
A buck, three does, and two little fawns.
They were playing around
And pawing the ground;
Their breath rose like steam
And it seemed like a dream
As I watched them butt heads and rub noses.

And then, as if by
Some silent command,
The entire band strolled right on over
And nibbled some twigs off my bushes and roses.
I watched as they drifted
Off into the night
And I thought to myself what a beautiful sight.

I like winter, though,
When I'm not shoveling snow;
There are no weeds to pull
And the grass doesn't grow --
No flowers to water,
No bugs on tomatoes,
No time wasted swatting gnats and mosquitoes.

I think the wild creatures
Enjoy winter too.
Their young are all grown
And there's not much to do
Except find enough food and shelter at night;
I'm sure God in His goodness will see it's done right.
And that's why I like this old winter thing --
But still, still, I look forward to spring.

Winter Never Looked So Good

Spring is here, the shrubs need pruning;

Tiller and mower need fine tuning.

Snow combined with bitter cold

Left my lawn with spots of mold.

See that peeling on the trim?

Must I paint the house again

And fix the crack in the foundation?

Well, there goes my spring vacation.

I raked the mulch off my rose bed,

Half of which it seems is dead,

And planted flowers in warm breezes --

Wouldn't you know, that night it freezes.

Garden rows in perfect order,

Slugs and bugs wait at the border,

Insecticide took my last dime --

Winter, come back anytime!

Law of the Jungle

The eyes glare blood red
And dart through the forest
As the swamp frogs sing
Their favorite old chorus.

Law of the jungle
Is not always nice.
The strong win the game;
The meek pay the price.

An aged and weak
Old Thomson's gazelle --
Her home, paradise,
But she lives in hell.

A lion from the brush --
It goes for her head;
Quick bite to the neck --
The Tommy is dead.

The pride gathers 'round
For their grisly feast
As first streaks of light
Now show in the east.

Appetites sated,
Bellies full of meat,
They seek forest shade
To escape the heat.

Law of the jungle --
That's how they survive.
The call of the wild
Helps keeps them alive.

The Eagle Soared

The eagle soared forth from her rocky rim
And screamed with delight as she raced with the wind,
Searching the ground with an arrogant stare,
Playing with gods of the pure mountain air.

Down below, concealed in a rock,
A poacher crouches with rifle cocked,
In plain site, a dead rabbit for bait --
Have a smoke, a beer, and sit and wait.

The eagle, enticed, goes into a dive;
Her future seems bright and so much alive.
Down she soars at breakneck speed;
Back at the nest there are mouths to feed.

She struggles with bait tied by a thong;
Too late she senses that something is wrong.
The rifle cracks a clean shot through the head,
And our symbol of freedom lies there dead.

The poacher with evil grin ponders his kill
And smiles at the thought of his pockets he'll fill.
Someone will pay big money to mount
And display the trophy -- without a doubt!

But across the valley a ranger sees all
Perched high above valley and timber wall;
To himself he mutters through the looking glass,
"You're in big trouble now, you stupid ass!"

He radios his partner to block the trail,
And the poacher becomes a guest in the jail.
Justice is swift -- guns taken away;
Add fines, plus jail time -- a year and a day.

The small orphaned birds are raised by hand,
Then rangers free them in native land.
The poacher who feels like a common thief
Decides, when released, to turn a new leaf.

Now he shoots with a camera instead of a gun
For a wildlife magazine; his heart was won!

Safe at Last

The doe said to her fawn,
"Let us fly like the wind.
We must get to that place,
To the home of our friend."

The fawn whimpered, "Why?
What is the reason?"
"Tomorrow's the start
Of deer hunting season!"

And so they ran
O'er hill and dale,
Meeting their kind
On well worn trail --

'Til they saw the place
With 'No Hunting' signs
Hanging on fences,
On line after line.

Spying orange jackets
Across the wide road,
They stayed in the woods
And kept their heads low.

Hunters were growling,
Cursing their luck;
No doe did they see,
And no ten-point buck.

Safe in their refuge
The deer were so glad;
Luck of the orange coats
They hoped was all bad.

They danced and they pranced
In cool autumn breeze,
Feasting on apples
That fell from the trees.

With pure spring water
And sweet tasting clover,
They were happy and safe
'Til the season was over.

Hunter and Hunted

The wolf peeks out of her hidden lair
Gingerly sniffing the cool night air;
Little ones sleep in their grassy nest,
She must go hunting and they must rest.

Off she trots to the farmer's yard,
Never once does she lower her guard.
Silently entering the poultry pen,
She grabs an old rooster and red speckled hen.

Breaking their necks with a single bite,
Back to the den in the gathering light.
When the farmer awakes at the crack of dawn
He goes out and finds that his chickens are gone.

He calls his dogs and loads his gun,
Away they go at a frenzied run.
Her wild heart is gripped with fear,
The barking dogs are growing near.

Leading them away from the den,
Off she goes on the run again.
Around in circles, 'cross the crick,
Fooling hounds with this ancient trick.

The baying curs are all confused,
Deceived again by clever ruse.
She lies panting in the sun --
Farmer: zero. She-wolf: one.

Footprints in the Snow

Where do all those footprints go
When warm spring sunshine melts the snow?
Chickadee tracks under the feeder,
Deer paths in the woods,
Following the leader as they go
Making their way through new fallen snow.

Where do they go? Where do they go,
The tracks of squirrel, the rabbit, the crow?
Where do they go? Where do they go?

Fox tracks made in hops and jerks,
Do tiny prints tell where the field mouse lurks?
All content in the nest of hay,
Is he the fox's lunch today?
The fox moves on, the scent is stale;
The mouse sleeps on in his broken bale.

When all those tracks disappear,
Are they filed away for use next year
When snow comes back and cruel winds blow?
Will we ever know? Will we ever know?

Battles and Blessings

Men never learn from past mistakes --
War doesn't give, it only takes.
Peace could last forevermore,
If only man would outlaw war.

Outlaw War

If only man would outlaw war
And nations vow to fight no more,
But such is a mere fantasy --
Mankind won't live in harmony.

Some countries have and some have not;
And one wants what the other's got.
Officers send out the orders;
Off they march across the borders.

God hears the fearsome battle cry;
The wounded scream and good men die.
Midst all of the mass destruction,
Someone plans for reconstruction.

Men never learn from past mistakes --
War doesn't give, it only takes.
Peace could last forevermore,
If only man would outlaw war.

A Rough Road

The road we trod is a rough road;
It's the same for you and for me.
The longer we live, the more we give
And we learn that nothing is free.

Politicians are crying, "More taxes!
Let's keep this great country on track!"
One hand they've got in our pockets
And the other one stabbing our backs.

Gone are the carefree days of yore,
When we lived off the fat of the land.
We made a buck, it was ours to keep,
And life was simple and grand.

Newt had better pull in his horns;
His Contract's an obvious trick.
He talks of a balanced budget
At expense of the old and the sick.

Don't mess with our Social Security!
That's ours to have and to hold.
We earned it, you son of a gun,
So don't leave us out in the cold.

America's still a great country;
Let's hope it always will be!
Our leaders should keep priorities straight
Down there in Washington, D.C.

The Military

Something about a babe
Asleep and safe in his crib
Stirs joy in a mother's breast.
Will he have to grow up
And march off to war
To be killed in some military quest?

Soldiers seem to thrive on war --
Is it just, to them, a task?
When the call comes down
They will rally around
Without any questions asked.

For the average man
It can ruin his plans;
And he knows it might hasten his end.
He'd rather be home with his wife and his kids,
Near his cat, his dogs, and his friends.

But we need the military, I guess;
Some of the reasons I see.
We want to be safe by day and by night
And dwell in the land of the free.

Simple Things

Have you ever noticed how little
Happiness there is in the world today?
People look so haggard and sad,
Papers are full of murder and rape,
And the news on TV is all bad.

Nobody sings when they work anymore,
They won't look you straight in the eye when they talk.
They glance all around and don't tip their hat
When taking the dog for a walk.
Well, what the hell, let's change all of that!

Let's hear the birds sing,
Let's hear the bells ring,
Let's start to wear feelings of glad --
It really can't be all that bad.

Little kids still play in their childish way,
And old men still sit in the park.
The sun shall shine and the weather's just fine,
And the stars will come out after dark.

If we only make room for the simple things
And follow a course true and steady,
We'll lose that sad feeling
And find life more appealing --
I know I'm feeling better already.

Reading the Signs

Will Rogers never met a man he didn't like,
Regardless of all who came down the pike.
But I've known some men that were meaner than sin,
With hearts of pure gall and no love for kin.

With minds that were evil and souls that were black,
They'd run you down flat and never look back.
They'd steal all you have, your home and your money,
Then wickedly curse you and think it was funny.

Some folks, on the other hand, come from good seed;
They stand by your side in times of your need,
Their voices are gentle, considerate, and kind
As they offer you comfort and give peace of mind.

You just have to learn to read all the signs,
Of the good hearted souls and the devilish minds.
Thank God for the friends that are faithful and true;
Those callous cads will someday get their due.

Dollars and Cents

Elections are over and I know we're all glad
To see the last negative TV ad.
Now we move on to more important events,
Things we relate to in dollars and cents.

As I continue this poet's discourse --
Of what am I speaking? Christmas, of course!
Hurry to the malls before it comes to an end;
Get out the checkbooks and spend, spend, spend!

Stretch to the limit that old credit card;
Buy worthless things for your house and your yard.
The babe in the manger, naked and cold?
That story doesn't make it -- it's gotten so old.

Forget the three wise men who followed the star;
If they did it today, they would drive a car.
Forget third world countries that hunger and thirst.
This is America! Our pleasure comes first.

So fill up the glass and have one more drink.
Merry Christmas to all -- I think.

Pen and Poetry

Alas, my paper stays totally blank;
It makes me so damn mad.
This writing life won't pay the rent
On this lonely little pad.

The Greatest Poet

I must have come from different times
'Cause I like poetry that rhymes.
I like the flowing of the words --
The adjectives, the nouns, the verbs.
And like the brook that's babbling,
The birds a-sailing on the wing,
The grass that sprouts up in the spring,
I also do the rhyming thing.
And so, my friends, I guess we know it,
Nature is the greatest poet.
Yes, I'm just a country boy
And so I find my greatest joy
Walking through the oaks and pines
Where I grew up with nature's rhymes.

My Poetry

My poems, I think, are better than most --
Ah, do I detect a note of scorn?
I've never been one given to boast,
But can I not once blow my own horn?

My poetry causes the thunder to roll
And lightning to streak 'cross the sky
Like a celestial light that brightens the night,
Like a power that rules from on high.

My poetry speaks for the common man,
Of his struggles, his hardships and strife,
And of how he does the best that he can
As he travels this journey of life.

You say my stuff is pretty bad,
And some of it's even worse?
Hell, it speaks for our times
And, by golly, it rhymes --
Is that the whole object of verse?

My mailbox fills with rejection slips,
Enough to paper my den.
But I go on writing these damnable rhymes
And go right on sending them in.

Topics of Love

I can't write about
Topics of love,
The passion, the heartache,
The stars up above,
That worn out line
About moon and June,
The billing and cooing
Of turtle doves.
I simply cannot
Make myself write
About topics of love,
Be it day or night.

Hey! Who am I
Trying to kid?
I can't write about love?
I think I just did.

A Dreamer

Oh, I'm going to write an epic poem!
It'll be a huge success, I know.
Words will leap from pen to paper
In an even steady flow.

Shall I write 'bout knights of old
Or dainty damsels in distress?
Perhaps the hardy pioneers
That tamed the old and wild west?

I will write a masterpiece,
A gripping story, all in rhyme!
No one will want to put it down
'Til they've read the final line.

Not able to print it fast enough --
That's how good it will sell!
I'll be on Oprah Winfrey
And Sally Raphael!

Alas, my paper stays totally blank;
It makes me so damn mad.
This writing life won't pay the rent
On this lonely little pad.

With a fresh brewed cup of coffee
And dash of milk from the creamer,
I'll rest my head and just kick back,
I'm a poet and a dreamer.

I Tried

I wrote a novel and sent in a copy.
The editor said, "It's written too sloppy."

I reworked the whole thing, this time their way.
The editor said, "Throw the damned thing away."

So I plagiarized others, I've just now attested.
The editor said, "I could have you arrested!"

Now what do I do? I'm all out of luck.
This writing is harder than driving a truck.

Write! Write! Write!

Staring at paper
So totally blank,
Days shrinking,
Street lights blinking,
Spirits sinking,
Voices whispering,
Write! Write! Write!

Cat rubs my leg,
Wants to be fed.
I try singing,
And humming,
Nothing coming,
Poor plumbing!
Write! Write! Write!

Cat goes out,
And at my desk
Great exaltation
And inspiration.
Words surging,
Cries of urging,
Write! Write! Write!

Eight hours straight,
Pounding out story,
Of romance and glory.
Send it away
The very same day
But until I see pay,
Write! Write! Write!

As expected,
The piece is rejected;
I'm so low,
I could be dead.
Get that idea
Out of my head!
Write! Write! Write!

Another call,
They want my work
After all.
Euphoric delight!
Sit down,
You miserable clown!
Write! Write! Write!

I Can't Write Today

I can't write today --
The words won't come.
My mind's gone blank.
Ho, hum! Ho, Hum!

Maybe tomorrow
I'll think up a rhyme.
If I don't, what the heck,
I've got plenty of time.

I'm certainly not
Writing for pay.
Who'd want to buy
This stuff anyway?

What's Left?

Is there anything left to write about?
Has everything been written --
Poems 'bout flowers and warm summer showers,
Poems about puppies and kittens?

I've read rhymes 'bout times when our country
Was young and when pioneers trekked 'cross the plain,
When wagons creaked and you couldn't hear yourself speak
In the pounding of heat and the crashing of rain.

Robert Service wrote of the Yukon's gold,
Of star studded nights and harsh winter cold.
In summer the valleys were matted with clover
As he cashed in his dust and spent it on lust
To go out the next day and start over.

The poems about war, its blood and its gore
And heroes that died in the fighting,
Songs of the sea, of the wild and the free --
It's all been put down in writing.

Is there much left to say that hasn't been said?
What's there to write that hasn't been written?
And yet when I think, "Egad! I've been had!"
I seldom can entertain quittin'.

Hard Writing

It's hard to write about a rose --
Blooming in my flower bed,
The aroma that delights the nose,
Pretty petals, pink and red,
It slumbers 'neath the winter snows.
It's hard to write about a rose.

It's hard to write about a wife --
The partner that you take for life,
Angry words you shouldn't have said,
Forgiven when you go to bed,
Times of joy, times of strife.
It's hard to write about a wife.

It's hard to write about a pet --
Who cares if she's just seen the vet?
She sits upon your favorite chair
And looks at you with icy stare,
Comes in at night all soaking wet.
It's hard to write about a pet.

It's hard to write about a friend --
He's by your side until the end,
Always there in time of need,
Asks no reward for his good deed,
He winks his eye when you have sinned.
It's hard to write about a friend.

A Holy Light

The writing life is what he chose,
But why he did, nobody knows.
He never made a decent rhyme;
He never sold a single line.

Down in the diner the chef is carving,
While he's upstairs slowing starving
Like a mangy beast in its filthy stall
As mice play tag inside the wall.

Out on the street there's song and mirth,
Inside there's naught but hell on earth.
His shaking hand fumbles the pen,
Is this atonement for his sin?

Then through the window black with grime
A holy light begins to shine.
And as he sits there all alone,
An angel comes and takes him home.

Youth and Old Age

Voices are calling, calling to me,
Voices that won't be still.
Climb that mountain, sail that sea --
And some day I probably will.

The Stranger

My thoughts go back across the years
To days when I was young --
The dashing youth, though quite uncouth,
The ever witty tongue.

Then middle age came by one day
And knocked upon my door.
The mirror betrayed my sagging face,
My gnarled hand and slowing pace.
The stranger knocking on my door
Told me that I was young no more.

But now I've reached the final phase
Of restless nights and drowsy days,
Sailing onward to the end
With aches and pains whene'er I bend.
Still there's more happiness than tears --
Oh, silver locks and golden years!

Voices Are Calling

Voices are calling, calling to me,
Voices that won't be still.
Climb that mountain, sail that sea --
And some day I probably will.

I was going to work one fine day
To a dead end job with dead end pay.
Thinking how little I really earned,
I kept driving to the point of no return.

Somewhere in Kansas my old car broke down
Right outside of a one-horse town.
I sold it for junk, put supplies in my pack,
Headed down the road, and never looked back.

I slept on the ground next to the rails,
I slept in piles of musty bales.
I slept in bars and abandoned cars,
And I slept in a lot of jails.

I worked for a time in a dusty coal mine;
For a while I drove an old bus.
But when I'd hear voices calling again
I could not ignore it -- the wanderlust.

At times I yearned for a woman's soft touch
And warmth of the hearth and the home.
With little ones playing on carpeted floor,
I'd have no compulsion to roam.

A home-cooked meal has a lot of appeal
When your aim is just to survive,
But I know I would never last very long
Working some job from nine to five

The wanderlust is a sacred trust;
It can main you and it can kill.
But the voices keep calling, calling to me,
Those voices that won't be still.

It's awfully cold and I'm getting old,
And it's so hard to climb that next hill.
So I lay down on the cold, cold ground
And the voices are finally still.

That's where they found me all curled up --
Of worldly things I left not a trace --
Just a nameless old man in a cruel harsh land
With a smile on my windburned face.

No longer trod by horses' hooves,
The sun-burned lad without his shoes,
The children walking home from school,
The saint, the sinner, and the fool.

Country Roads

A country road is a fickle thing --
Dusty in summer, muddy in spring,
In winter months all cloaked with snow,
Still getting you where you want to go.

I live beside a country road,
On it I've hauled so many a load --
Racks of hay all sweet and fine,
Oats and wheat at harvest time,
Corn of burnished, yellow gold,
More than all the cribs could hold.

They're getting fewer every day
With metro expansion on the way.
The commuter in his shiny car
Wants to drive to work on tar.

No longer trod by horses' hooves,
The sun-burned lad without his shoes,
The children walking home from school,
The saint, the sinner, and the fool,
My country road will soon be gone
And so will I before too long.

The Farmstead

The farmstead is abandoned now,
With empty barn and idle plow.
Owners walked along the streams
And gazed across their field of dreams.
Now they stand there, man and wife,
As sun sets on a way of life.
Developers have bought the land
And propose pretentious plan.
One hundred homes will dot those fields
That once were lush with bumper yields
Of golden grain and new mown hay
That filled the farmer's busy day.
They'll grade and pave and bulldoze trees,
But they can't erase the memories.

Sweet Youth

Oh, to go back
To twenty-one,
When everything,
Even work, was fun.
Sweet youth,
Glowing good health,
Vigor and vim --
Oh, to be
Twenty-one again.

In glorious days
Of flaming youth,
We thirsted for knowledge
And hungered for truth.

Under the cloak
Of life's magic spell,
We freely drank from
Life's bottomless well.

But youth fades like dew
In the morning sun,
And one day we awake
To find it all gone.

Gone are the hopes
And dreams that we had;
Gone are the plans,
The good with the bad.

Some battles were lost
And some were won --
Oh, to go back
To twenty-one.

Virtuous Three

The old man said to the passing youth,
"Where do you go in such haste?"
"I'm searching for honesty, love, and truth,
And I haven't a moment to waste."

The old man gave a cynical laugh,
And he said, "Why, haven't you heard?
Honesty and truth have long since died,
And love is a four-lettered word."

The youth ignored the old man's words
As he continued on at a run
With head held high and a glint in his eye
To the east and the rising sun.

At last he came to a bend in the road
And there in a shady nook
A maiden sat with a babe on her lap
And they had an angelic look.

As he gazed at the pair in the cool morning air,
He knew that he'd found all three.
This innocent maid with the gurgling babe
Were truth and love and honesty.

Falling Chips

The New Year's here; the old one's gone.
Let's celebrate with drink and song,
Numb our brains with wine and rum
And winsome thoughts of days to come.

Will I be blessed with glowing health,
With fame and happiness and wealth?
Or will I sink to misery
And join the ranks in poverty?

I'll let the chips fall where they may
And live my life from day to day.
I'll try to do my level best,
Approach each task with zeal and zest.

And with the year gone, I'll look back
At my straight and narrow track.
I'll take the good and bad in stride
While keeping faith upon my side.

I know what e'er will be will be;
I hope the New Year's good to me.

Laid Up

Were you ever laid up
With a cold or the flu --
You mope 'round the house
With nothing you can do?

Your nose and eyes run --
Could fill up a lake;
You can't get to sleep
And you can't stay awake.

Should you go to the doctor?
Would that be the best?
He'll say, "You take aspirin
And get lots of rest."

Should you work tomorrow
Or call in sick?
Everybody will say
That's an old trick.

So to keep up my strength
I'll eat chocolate candy,
Use the ol' heating pad
And drink lots of brandy.

I'm too sick to cook;
I'll order Kentucky.
I might make this last
A whole month if I'm lucky.

A Gift

Life isn't always a bowl of cherries --
It can be just the pits.
Some days we'd like to chuck it all,
Throw in the towel and call it quits.

Then with a smile she says thank you
In a way that is truly sincere.
There's a big sunburst and the clouds disperse
And you know you're glad to be here.

When you're feeling low -- believe me, I know --
You can tire of life's endless quest.
You're down as far as you can go;
You couldn't be more depressed.

So then you recall good times gone by
And think of good times yet to come.
You see that life's not as bad as you thought --
Do you agree with me, my old chum?

One thing I've learned is to laugh at life;
When I do it gives me a lift.
I thank God for the days He has given me,
And I treasure each one as a gift.

An Old Man's Prayer

Lord, I've reached biblical three score and ten,
The traditional life span of women and men.
My fate's in Your hand, I bow to Your will
With hope that the rest won't all be downhill.

In Your goodness and mercy, please be kind,
Let me have health of body and mind
And also financial security --
I don't want to burden society.

In this the autumn of my life,
Keep me free from pain and strife,
Keep my eyes from growing weak,
Let me hear when people speak.

Time on earth is growing short,
But when I hear, "You must report,"
I'll wipe away those salty tears
And thank You for these golden years.

Then through the window black with grime,
A holy light begins to shine.
And as he sits there all alone
An angel comes and takes him home.

About the Author

From whence cometh this man who, in his "golden years," turned to pen and paper to soothe and satisfy? He comes from the land. He comes from a farm near Jordan, Minnesota -- a small community about a half hour southwest of the Twin Cities. It is on the farm that Jesse Coghill acquired the roots of a country man and the soul of a poet. It is where he continues to find comfort, contentment, and time for contemplation.

His childhood gave early indication that Jesse would remain a man of the land, of the farm. He was not comfortable, for example, within the confines and constraints of the elementary parochial school in Jordan. Although the young student gravitated toward English and Geography, he preferred Recess -- and the freedom of the countryside where he could "walk along the streams and gaze across a field of dreams."

He preferred fishing on the river bottoms of Sand Creek, about a mile straight west of the farm, where he, his older brother Jim, and neighbor boys congregated after completion of chores. "We'd fish for a while and then we'd go skinny dipping," says Jesse. "We fished for bullheads and carp while they were still young and sweet. The carp -- we'd let the chickens eat them. Chickens didn't like old carp, and we didn't like old bullheads."

The country boy even preferred hoeing thistles from the cornfields to classroom work. "I didn't mind the thistles," he says. "We got paid for hoeing them -- and we'd spend it all on firecrackers for the Fourth of July. We made cannons out of pipes and blew up tin cans. Jim almost cut off his toe one time. I told him he'd still have nine left so quit worrying about it. It was only his little toe anyway."

High school days at Jordan Public were a bit more comforting to the freedom-seeking lad. "It was like getting out of prison after being in parochial school," he says. In thinking upon those four years of study, Jesse said, "I wish I'da taken up typing. I wanted to, but it was all girls in the class. Girls were sharp in that sort of thing, it seemed, and I guess I was self-conscious." In his youth, the drive to get words on paper was not strong enough to overcome shyness.

So Jesse found comfort in Shop class, where a man could properly work with his hands. Such comfort, however, did not lead to expertise in things mechanical. LaVerne Coghill says of her husband, who now rents their farm acreage to others, "He fixed his own farm machinery until he ran out of wire or duct tape." As a matter of fact, the non-mechanical country man lost two fingers to the grinding gears of a corn-picker. "That happened the same year Kennedy was shot," said Jesse. "I was old enough to know better."

***

Born on August 23rd, 1926, at "Dr. Fisher's Hospital" in Shakopee, Minnesota, Jesse was the fourth of eight children begotten by Donald and Elizabeth Coghill.

"I was twelve pounds," says Jesse. "I was overdue about a month. I almost died so was baptized immediately. It was some kind of kidney trouble. I was baptized Jesse Francis -- Francis after my grandfather Francis Coghill. I never knew him. One of my brothers -- Little Joe, we always called him -- died at birth. He was a blue baby. I think that meant no circulation and heart problems. Today that's correctable."

Jesse's parents were not of German ancestry as were most of their neighbors. Elizabeth Coghill, with a maiden name of Smith, was English. "She was a prim and proper lady," says Jesse. "She was Victorian -- like the old Queen Victoria -- and very religious, but she could play the piano a little and she had a sense of humor."

"My dad was Scottish," continued Jesse, "and he had a great sense of humor, too, but he was never well. When he was young he had rheumatic fever, which he never fully recovered from. He was a hard worker, but awkward as hell. He couldn't fix anything. He wired everything. But he was a good horseman. He always claimed he was an exercise boy for the famed Dan Patch. Maybe he was a dreamer and would like to have been. But maybe he really was that exercise boy. Sometimes, after we say things often enough, it becomes reality."

Jesse said his dad loved baseball and, prior to the kids developing that similar interest, Donald Coghill would attend baseball games on Sunday afternoons while his kids went to the movies.

"My dad died before I got out of high school," said Jesse, "so I had to work on this damn farm and support my mother and three younger sisters. It's not that I didn't like the farm, but I had wanted to join the navy for a while. Anyhow, I graduated in 1944 -- the same year my dad died. He died in April at the age of fifty. We were still using horses for a couple more years. With the war on, nobody was producing tractors. When they became available, I bought my first tractor. That was in 1946. I didn't have to drive those smelly horses anymore. I didn't have to look at those horses' asses all day."

One fine day, when the horses were history, a young girl by the name of LaVerne Picha, with roots in the nearby community of New Prague, entered the life of Jesse Coghill. "She was in the park one afternoon and barefoot, and I picked a thorn out of her foot -- and she followed me around ever since. It was love at first sight." A thorn from a young lady's foot? "Actually, the first time I saw her she was driving around with her brother and their car conked out. I started it for her." After two years of courtship, which were, perhaps, more poetic than their first encounter, Jesse and LaVerne became man and wife. The date was August 5th, 1950. The place was St. John the Baptist Catholic Church in Jordan. The presiding priest was Jesse's brother, Jim -- who had, by that time, become Father Elstan Coghill, O.F.M.

The newlyweds made their home on the Coghill farm and, after a couple of years in the old farm house, built a modest new home on the place. It is still their home today, but they now leave tilling of the soil -- except for large patches of vegetable and flower gardens -- to others.   Their three children, who married and left home long ago, live and work nearby. Bruce is a maintenance man at Rosemount Engineering in Eden Prairie. Sheila Tammaro is an English professor at Moorhead State University. Mark works in the Aerospace Department at Rosemount Engineering in Burnsville.

***

When did Jesse take up writing? "About five or six years ago," he replied. "I've always wanted to write. It's easier for me to express my thoughts in written rather than spoken words. LaVerne and I do some traveling, gardening, and bird watching, but we don't play cards, we don't dance, and we don't drink -- so I decided to write. I've written lots of humorous short stories about the depression years and the '40's when I was growing up, but I especially like poetry. I've read a lot of poetry and liked the stories it told. I like Robert Burns, Robert Service, Poe and Longfellow -- all those old dudes. I like lots of British and American verse."

Is there a particular time between his sunrises that is more conducive to writing? "I write when the spirit moves me," he said, a bit embarrassed to admit a sentimental spirit, a calling voice, within his common country self. "Sometimes I don't write for a month, then maybe two or three poems in a couple days. I don't want to be a slave to it."

What gives him his greatest pleasure? "The farm -- the independence of being out in the middle of it and not next to anybody else -- and, now, freedom. I'm not running the farm anymore and that gives me freedom -- freedom to write, to enjoy good music and good food. And I like dogs and cats. I like all animals and birds."

If not a farmer, what might Jesse have been? "Maybe a blacksmith," he said. "I used to hang around the blacksmith shop in Jordan when my farm machinery broke down, and that was all very interesting."

This editor thinks the farmer might have been, not a black-smith, but a fisherman -- casting his line from sunrise to sunrise, listening to voices in the swells and swoons of nature, marveling at the poetry all about him, enjoying the calm waters and surviving the rough waters -- as Jesse would say, "just a nameless old man in a cruel harsh land with a smile on my windburned face."

Thank you, Jesse Coghill -- oh, poet, dreamer, and rebel -- for quiet time with calling voices.

*-- **Editor Sue***